Brooklynwinded

James Poulos

DEDICATION

I dedicate this book to Nikki, Katherine, and George who all met me here in Brooklyn and reflect the perfect joy that is within me.

CONTENTS

ACKNOWLEDGMENTS

I would like to acknowledge all the seekers of kindness and love, all our ancestors, my readers, my supporters on Instagram, and TikTok, and everyone who has crossed my path and enriched my life. Thank you to Nikki for her invaluable support with all my creative projects and to George and Katherine for being a constant source of inspiration and joy. Thank you to Amazon KDP for making creative expression accessible to more people.

1 THANX

I want to thank you so much
it bleeds
I want to thank you so much
it's corny
Like weeds.
I want to thank you so much
it burns
But I won't
Cause
I Don't

I want you to know so much
I'm more than careful
I keep my mouth closed
FERME
My hand far away
And I just glance at you
in the right way
I look right at you
and say
THANK YOU
Without a word
Without moving
Without anything

Except you'll know the truth
That
I feel about you
I want you to know
I'M GRATEFUL
I say thank you
Inside
Deep in a prayer that doesn't end
Incessantly repeating
THANK YOU
all day long
and you'll know.

You will feel
the wind on your skin
the magic inside
you will feel
that
I'm saying, 'Thank You'
Inside.
it's private
you know
It works better in prayer
Than with silly words.

"Thank You"
Even in silence
It's okay
The gratitude
You'll feel it at once.

2 RAIN

Downpour that's going on in each mind
The rain falling from the clouds
A reminder of it coming out of the brain
Creativity from our hands
Drops of words in books
like this
And like all books
this book
IS A GLIDE
you are the story unfolding
As the
Reading of words is done.
transferring to another place.

Without that thing
that everyone
Knows ...
what it is ...
But can't talk about
because it's sacrosanct.
And is there a special spell check,
For certain kinds of
words?

Brooklynwinded

Have you ever tried to do reiki in the rain
Inside
With windows down
Clapping booms
And
Flashing Light
dark midafternoon.

Brooklynwinded

it starts
to rain different
one day
And you see everything in some other way
Unimagined before
Now
you understand how to appreciate
Where you are in some mysterious way
Waking up happens
Now
Is happening
Right here . . . right day

Brooklynwinded

Suddenly
The morning sheets are warmly
Ruffled
king size bed for two
With a downtown city view
Liberty
Solid steel trains
Running underground

Brooklynwinded

Non-stop
Precise, hard, and loud
Waking from another land
Pushing sheets away
To stand
The ending of
Another day.

Dear rain
always here
bright sunshine
have all
everything
NOW
AM

Dear rain
it seems I
Have
An
Obsession with you, as much as with
The STARS
The MOON
And space
The Air
TREES
PEOPLE CLOSE TO ME

Dear rain
I
Have
An
Obsession
With
Your Clouds
And The Sky
You seem to rain from.

Dear rain
I have a hopeless split devotion
Because
The Ocean
The Sand
The mountains
The cats
Technology
The food we eat
I'm so desirous
Of
PEACE, LOVE, AND TRUTH.

Finally, dear rain
I must share
My love for you
Dear ribbons and candy
Falling from the sky
As I continue
In the now that is forever,
Being courageous in pursuit of . . .
Truth and freedom . . .
THINKING
Keep doing, keep being,
KEEP GOING.

Brooklynwinded

How awesome
Brilliant cloudburst
Leaving us with such a flood
WET
Soaked
Sopping
Drenched
Simply
SOG

Brooklynwinded

Perhaps dear rain
You can wash my mind
AWESOME
The brilliant mind
Magic dust or stars?
SPARKLING
Radiating cool.

Power thoughts
God running forth
Niagara Falls

Mathematical Genius
Creative Magic
Explaining
Building the world

Heart craving
Crying to influence
Scientific politic.

Brooklynwinded

Savvy, sharp, socialite
Turning motion
Selling art

Awesome brilliant mind
Miraculous gifted
Form of God

Faithful heart
Fearful prisoner of illusion

However

Rain sets us free.

And my breath merges with the rain
And all is abandoned to its tempest
perpetual grey . . .
And
Unexpectedly
It stops
rain stops falling
And
In the bright sun
Wonderment
Thinks
Where is the rain?
That moment of mystical quiet
No rain
No wind
Only air.

Brooklynwinded

The rain has stopped
And
Unexpectedly
There is a space
Even in the sun
Left empty
Now that the rain
Has gone
Somewhere else
For now.

Thank you
Thanks
Thanks so much
I am so grateful
I cannot find the words to express my gratitude
Thank you, thank you, thank you
thank you very much
THANKS A MILLION
many thanks
I really appreciate it

3 TRUTH

Spent a while learning about truth
Wanting to know what it is
How it looks
Where to find it
Does somebody know?
Factually
Basically
There is only one truth
That can be explained in words . . .

The only truth that can be proven and agreed upon unanimously, therefore making it the absolute truth, is that there are miscellaneous opinions about everything, and this is the one absolute truth in this physical world.

Opinions about everything
One kind of truth
Yes
Doesn't stop the search.
FOR
When I visit a tree
The way it talks
the message in the leaves
the trunk . . . The bark . . .
The direction of its lean
This is a kind of truth
Mystery unseen.

Brooklynwinded

Does each of us
Grapple with the meaning of truth?
Tell, what you think
Who operates this machine?
Are there controls?
Can we drop our bodies out of our souls?
For just a moment
To catch a glimpse?

Brooklynwinded

Truth hovers
I see its mist
Around some tracks
Like a morning dew
Without moisture
Soulless
On the next round
I merge with it again
A sigh of relief
There's FORTUNE
At the controls.

Fortune
Doesn't speak
A silent ride operator
Vaster than
The ocean.

Many opinions in One Universe
I am that
I am I
Awareness is
Has always been
will forever be
TRUTH IS.

Human body robot
Mechanic mind
TRUTH
GOD
AWARENESS
Awareness takes human form
Human form experiences things
Human form and experiences come and go.
Awareness remains.

Brooklynwinded

Write from this perspective
(of truth)
But how?
Without describing
An experience . . .
Like a wordless rose bush does not
Describe an experience
Rather . . .
Just to be next to a rose bush
Just be next to a beautiful friend
And understanding arrives.

Brooklynwinded

Can words come close to truth
Or
Do they just come very close
Until I can be truth
And forget
The meaning of beauty.

Can SILENCE come close
to TRUTH?
Until it can be Truth?
And forget Love.
Can kindness come close
to
TRUTH
Until it can be truth
And forget kindness?

The truth is that there are a lot of varying opinions about every topic and at the place where there is no opinion is where lies the TRUTH . . . and there, is found absolute kindness . . . the type of kindness with indescribable beauty . . . and that beauty is agreed upon by all, and this unanimity is the unspeakable beautiful indestructible invincible truth.

All can feel this beauty when the only appropriate response to beauty is silence. When there is no other response other than beauty itself, TRUTH is witnessed.

Brooklynwinded

Silence
This morning's silence
Last night wailing throughout
Outside today . . . sounds of prayer . . .
Inside
Finding each other in the beautiful sky
The color of love.

Brooklynwinded

The
truth showing itself to me
At this moment of my now
Is the incredible chaos of
How many opinions
Are vying for the trophy of reality
When
The actual truth is inside the
kind silence that nurtures and loves
protects and supports.

OPINIONS

What lies between opinions that
Keep this world functional?
Despite the presence of constant variations
And wrestling between views . . .
is a common ground . . .
Like God
INDESCRIBABLE.

Brooklynwinded

Discovery
I came across a lie
It felt icy
A strange wind across my viewfinder
Preventive action
A feeling of immediate awareness
Shook my self
And told me
That there was a better place than this
And that is where I go
So there
is where I am.

Brooklynwinded

Delicious how truth
offers a better place
I see it
So
I start walking towards it
Towards
Freedom
And
I know it is
The only road to take.

Many kindly souls
Reflect what we know
Like a philosopher
Explaining human truth
Indicating that
Truth
Is really
On our mind

Brooklynwinded

Having truth on the mind
Is a high vibration
So beautiful
The essence of truth
I seek it every moment
The very seeking of it
Pure air.
I look for it in my wife, my family,
In vases, in people's aura,
In nature
Everywhere.

I am grateful for this desire to understand
the truth
the core of universal spirit and oneness
that many call God.
The connection with the first glimpse into reality.
TRUTH

Thoughts about truth clarify. Truth as awareness increases
as the world is observed in an objective fashion. Language
is an endowment with which we choose to communicate
and speak or state truth … and it seems that words may
alter reality and events of reality in some form, even if we are
unconscious. It appears that the meaning attached to
words, along with each word or group of words' vibration
affects physical reality. Unseen reality is also affected by
thought and words.

Can someone lie to themselves? Does the mechanism of lying affect the
person performing the untruth? Is a lie an
experiment to understand the truth? What is the truth?

4 LOOK

I don't look down
Don't look if it's your wont
Look down there's some pennies
Look down when I won't
Look down at our hands
See that sidewalk
Those nice shoes
I look down
And I won't
Don't speak my mind
Until you ask

Brooklynwinded

Look down to stop time
Go all around town with you
Past shops and corners past parks
Just looking down
Look down cause you're fun
Look down to get level
Stairs ahead
Climbing up looking down again
Love you ahead
Looking down staying even
Not sure what I know
The only time I look up is to see you.
Don't have much to speak

Brooklynwinded

Cause there's no way to say it
Don't have much to display
There's no way to show it
Not anything to explain
You just got to know it
Get going, get moving
No looking, asking, or groping
You are here today and now
You are forever.
No explanation
I feel you and know it
I get it
I love it
I am it.

Textbook at the Candy Store
Brooklyn mystic
There's many Brooklynz
But this one
$&@f$;@
You know

Brooklynwinded

It's so old and dark
Just catching a train
Coffee in the air
unseen stars and lots of rain
Staid hipster how do you figure
It got all about here
Don't know what it's about
But it's all energy and sneakers.

Devotional Direction
There's no need to explain and to verify
Thinking explanations can soothe and glorify
They can be misunderstood
So
No need to ask
Nothing turns away
It's all now
It sounds like lore
It's all plain
There's no hack
Quite simply
Many people are quite free.

No need to go back or keep moving forward
there's no lack in the NOW
the key is here
it's cold out there
warm inside.

Look for the universal silence that's always here.
Thoughts running like a wild river, thoughts so fast can bury
the beauty of silence. Beautiful Truth can pause the rough
currents of pain and fear. Look for soft shadows that are not
real yet helpful. A beautiful shadow can quiet the mind. How
nice to have a tranquil mind, especially when there is awareness
of the universe within.

Mind wants to go the intellectual route, to ask, to understand,
to evaluate, however, the heart knows that there is no
clear answer outside of the Truth, and the Truth is already
here, now and it is important to be thankful and watchful
while going through life. Daily mindfulness practice improves
awareness and the temptation to engage in falseness will go away.

Sometimes there is a current of wild thinking and it is at this time that I ask,
"Are these thoughts contributing to chaos?
Perhaps it is better to meditate, to read, or better yet to simply observe …
without judgement."

Brooklynwinded

Where is the silence?
In the space between the blinds
Under the plate
Behind the couch
Inside your socks
At the bottom of your dresser
In a drawer.

Brooklynwinded

Mystic desire to be the change I seek
My wounds find expression in
English
For my ancestors
For my world
Gesture of love
Desire for unity
Global citizenship
I want to be One
I don't know which language it is
As long as we feel it, right.

In case you forget, take a moment to remember
how beautiful you are
because you are, quite beautiful.

Brooklynwinded

Sometimes poetry doesn't come in words
So I watch
I am a lighthouse
Ready
For that beauty
To come sailing in
And when I find it
Mmmmmm
It's better than a perfectly crafted
Dark chocolate square.

Brooklynwinded

I take everything metaphorically
And it is not because I'm wrong
I saw a glitch in the boundary
Between the here and there
Saw it too early
To just hang and play
I watch and wonder
Love to pray.

5 POETRY

Poetry
Like a fresh breeze
A nice sneeze
Poetry
A friend
A balm
A protector
A guarantee
Just like spring water
Poetry
It's for you and me
A true reflection
of our humanity.

Victorious poetry
Working to perfect
The flaws of reality
Each word
Each line
Each stanza
Each page
Each book
A step closer
To
What really is.

Great

Poetry

Sings

The

Truth

Brooklynwinded

A page can be turned
Whenever you are ready
So don't linger
As time
Moves forward
Space is revealed
And haunting silence fills the chest
Rain pulls down the lungs
Life vanishes from here
Showing us
We've been in the wrong place
All along.

Brooklynwinded

Every morning upon arising
I'm awestruck
We are still here.
This is still happening?
MIRACLE
I live with constant gratitude of life's survival.
With how many factors required to live
How can it be that one could even breath
This must be an illusion
Or mere buffoonery
Nevertheless,
I say, "THANK YOU"

Brooklynwinded

A poet
lived only during the night
he wrote
by an open window
every morning
at 1am
with deep breath
and
nothing in the way
dark 4am crystal wind
freedom
magic pen.

Poetry is the pulse of life
and the robust energy of a poem
always bursts forth from gratitude.
Please take a moment and enjoy the gratitude you
have towards this beautiful world you are in.
Think of any one thing you are grateful for
and write a gratitude poem on the next page.
If you can't compose a poem, simply fill the page
with the phrase:

Thank You

6 TEMPORARY CONCLUSION

Here starts the temporary conclusion, awkwardly referred to often, as the end is really the beginning.

Ideas can be thought of as ideas when they are analyzed with words and through the mind.

Brooklynwinded

thoughts without awareness
can be
constructs
of a confident human mind.

Brooklynwinded

Shadows
there are no longer any shadows
on enlightened walks home
larger shadows have been cast
by a cover of clouds over NYC

The entire ground dull
no shadow walking below
no shadow under gate or tree
no shadow under lamppost
or tables left on the curb.

Brooklynwinded

Shadows

However, under cars
there are dark shadows
portals
to the world unseen
Then
suddenly, a pot of yellow daffodils
owned by another
stirs a great feeling of admiration in me.

I WANT

to talk
An urge
Will each word open up a world once hidden?
like a volcanic ashy wind
words are
formulations of thoughts
reflections of inner reality
attempts to truth.

LIFE

We are visitors
We are human
We are actors
We are egos
We are dreamers
We are seekers
We are finders
We are saints
We are One.

LIFE

Brooklynwinded

Abandoned Motels

abandoned motel
nothing inside
don't want to go
sell it
raze it
it's gone away
motel now a flat piece
land of grassy weed
goodbye abandoned motel
body in this land is broken free

just falling asleep
trying to get through
opaque windows and climbing
mountains I've thought up myself. I
love to pray
nevertheless prayers fall asleep
and truth continues to exist. I fly with wings made of
awareness and I see it all and know
it's right next to me and the more I slow down the brain the
more I see.

Brooklynwinded

keep on getting so much it's in front of me, I don't need to
ask
I am the dream I have

But I'm tired of tripping and stumbling
until I get proof

that's stubborn

so I let it go and that's when it's all truth.

Fighting monster
shaped as sleep
can't stay up
I'm falling through
keep holding on
for me
for you.

Brooklynwinded

So narrated
and life never ends
what a realization that this presence will always be
here
like it is now
and this now is forever
and what with the body
what will it do
its attachment to the soul
is quite peculiar
how it causes sensation of some
sort
oh how it feels
to just
be
to simply sit
to walk
to eat
to think
to eat
to think
to live.

Brooklynwinded

7 WILDFLOWER

Wildflower love
love is life
is truth
is all
Love, love, love
because with it there is truth
I shall find a meadow
and know
how to be
eternal
because here I'm always with you.

Brooklynwinded

time sweeps by
and scrapes my heart
tells me
nothing stands still
this earthly plane
is perfect
and when I know this
never back again
ready for purity
wings of love
strength of truth
beauty absolute.

Brooklynwinded

By writing this
I've actually broken my own attempt
of being and nothingness
because of desire to share
this experience
I've negated the very exercise I've set out to accomplish:
To practice getting better at doing nothing.

The hopeless song of words
describes beauty
and
simultaneously makes it disappear.

Meditation may be the essential component of an actual birth. Born on earth is a challenge to the intellect. Perhaps this puzzle is necessary in order to emerge as a member of this universal constituency. However, when all pursuits are material, physical, and ego based the person is nothing more than a machine carrying a soul that will not emerge in this lifetime. Luxury is good but luxury with awareness is better. This achievement of uniting with the universe is the accomplishment of beauty, the finding of truth, and the manifestation of everlasting joy.

My guides are appropriately mystic, nothing like what I would expect intellectually. Therefore, with honesty I pursue truth . . . growing in faith I learn to live by heart, and I find joy one revelation at a time.

A cessation of complaining is a vital first step towards ascension. My reflections have provided a tremendous amount of support to which I am absolutely grateful. By reflections, I mean that, everything I see out there is merely an extension of the reality that I have created in my mind. Through complex personalities and relationships to them I have come to realize that the only way to be grateful is to strive to understand the complexities inherent in this relationship between the inner self and the outer world.

Reflection . . . I will observe your inner demons until you are completely expelled. You shall be observed steadily until Truth emerges cloudless. This is success. We are stardust and together we make up the world.

The only truth that I have discovered is that the only truth that exists is that there is an abundance of Opinion. When I try to disprove this "opinion as truth" theory, in order to see its wisdom, I come across an intersection that feels like friction. It may be that at some point, where all individual beings are in complete agreement with each other and there are no opposing opinions, there is a movement beyond seeking for truth, beyond truth itself, and this may be One, whole undivided UNIVERSE.

8 MEADOW JOURNAL

It is my hope and intention that this book will inspire you to journal and appreciate joy. Please use all the pages of this book to have gratitude for the joy that you are or to show the appreciation for the joy that you are discovering. Write and scribble away with joy.

Throughout the Meadow Journal you will find some sweet words and phrases.

WEEDS ARE FLOWERS

CONSIDERATION

TRANQUILITY

ELEGANT

MIRACLE

PEACE

SANGUINE

CHERISH TRUTH

EARTH

SUN

STARS

ELEVATED

MINDFUL

CARING

TRUTHFUL

EMPOWERING

Brooklynwinded

WINNER

YOU ARE SIGNIFICANT

YOU ARE IMPORTANT

NOW

YOU ARE TIMELESS

YOU ARE A TREASURE

APPRECIATION

YOU ARE BEAUTIFUL

BEAUTY IS YOU

THANK YOU

I LOVE YOU

SPREAD JOY

YOU INSPIRE KINDNESS

YOU ARE A STAR

MAY YOU FIND YOUR TREE

YOU ARE SO AWARE

LIKE YOGA

SUCH NOURISHMENT

YOU ARE UNIVERSE

STARDUST

INFINITY

WISDOM

SHINE

DIAMONDS

CHEERS

TOGETHER

SPIRIT

TRANSCENDENCE

Brooklynwinded

SUPPORT

EXQUISITE

Brooklynwinded

TRUTH

YOU ARE IMPORTANT

ANGELS ARE EVERYWHERE

COURAGE

FRIEND

SELF

ENLIGHTENED

DIVINITY

ENERGY

PURITY

FOREVER

KINDNESS

Brooklynwinded

PRAYER

LISTEN

HEALTH

HAPPINESS

PROTECTION

FORGIVEN

RESPECT

FLOWERS ARE WEEDS

9 FLY

Each word
seems a seed
convinced
the beautiful garden is planted
invisible thoughts
in the ground
watered

while the wait to bloom
goes through seasons
and time's shadows appear
in
Spring
Summer
Fall
Winter

all is weed
but the TRUTH
flowers

ABOUT THE AUTHOR

James Poulos was born in Brooklyn, New York. His work seeks to understand spiritual values and contribute to the increasing of human awareness. He enjoys travel with his wife and getting together with family and friends.

Made in United States
North Haven, CT
10 March 2024

49769467R00088